RAINTREE BIOGRAPHIES

Abraham Lincoln

Michael V. Uschan

A Harcourt Company

Austin New York

www.raintreesteckvaughn.com

Published by Raintree Steck-Vaughn Publishers, an imprint of Steck-Vaughn Company.

Project Editors: Sean Dolan, Leigh Ann Cobb, Gianna Williams
Production Manager: Richard Johnson
Designed by Ian Winton

Planned and produced by Discovery Books

Library of Congress Cataloging-in-Publication Data

ISBN 0-7398-5678-2

Printed and bound in China
1 2 3 4 5 6 7 8 9 0 07 06 05 04 03 02

Acknowledgments
The publishers would like to thank the following for permission to reproduce their pictures:
Cover: Corbis; p. 4 Peter Newark's American Pictures; p. 5 Corbis; p. 6 Peter Newark's American Pictures; p. 7 The Stapleton Collection/Bridgeman Art Library; p. 8 Mary Evans Picture Library; p. 9 Chicago Historical Society/Bridgeman Art Library; pp. 10 & 11 Peter Newark's American Pictures; p. 12 Mary Evans Picture Library; p. 13 Peter Newark's American Pictures; p. 14 Mary Evans Picture Library; p. 15 New York Historical Society/Bridgeman Art Library; p. 16 Hishhorn Museum/Bridgeman Art Library; pp. 17, 18 & 19 Peter Newark's American Pictures; p. 20 top & bottom Corbis; p. 22 Peter Newark's American Pictures; p. 23 Corbis; p. 24 Peter Newark's American Pictures; p. 25 Corbis; p. 26 top Corbis; p. 26 bottom Mary Evans Picture Library; p. 27 Peter Newark's American Pictures; p. 28 Corbis; p. 29 Peter Newark's American Pictures. Map by Stefan Chabluk.

Dedication
With love to Imari, Mikey, Madison, and Tahitia.
Uncle Mike.

Contents

Keeping America Free

The Gettysburg Address is one of the shortest speeches any president ever gave, yet it includes some of the most poetic language any president ever spoke. On November 19, 1863, Abraham Lincoln dedicated a cemetery at the battlefield at Gettysburg, Pennsylvania, for soldiers who died in the ongoing Civil War.

Lincoln's Gettysburg Address

November 19, 1863

Four score and seven years ago our fathers brought forth on this continent, a new nation, conceived in liberty, and dedicated to the proposition that all men are created equal.

Now we are engaged in a great civil war, testing whether that nation, or any nation so conceived and so dedicated, can long endure. We are met on a great battle-field of that war. We have come to dedicate a portion of that field, as a final resting place for those who here gave their lives that that nation might live. It is altogether fitting and proper that we should do this.

But, in a larger sense, we can not dedicate – we can not consecrate – we can not hallow – this ground. The brave men, living and dead, who struggled here have consecrated it, far above our poor power to add or detract. The world will little note, nor long remember what we say here, but it can never forget what they did here. It is for us the living, rather, to be dedicated here to the unfinished work which they who fought here have thus far so nobly advanced. It is rather for us to be here dedicated to the great task remaining before us – that from these honored dead we take increased devotion to that cause for which they gave the last full measure of devotion – that we here highly resolve that these dead shall not have died in vain – that this nation, under GOD, shall have a new birth of freedom – and that government of the people, by the people, for the people, shall not perish from the earth.

Although Lincoln spoke in a high-pitched voice, his words had great power. At Gettysburg, Lincoln held his audience spellbound with this written address.

A New Purpose

In the Gettysburg Address, Lincoln said victory would mean "that these dead shall not have died in vain—that this nation, under God, shall have a new birth of freedom—and that government of the people, by the people, for the people, shall not perish [die] *from the earth."*

Lincoln's brief speech, only lasting two minutes, did more than honor heroic soldiers who died in battle. Lincoln explained that the Union needed to win to uphold the ideals of freedom and democracy on which the nation had been founded, and to give birth to a new freedom.

SLAVERY IN THE U.S.

The first slaves were brought to North America from Africa in 1619. By the middle of the 19th century, the northern states were developing industry, while the southern states depended on agriculture. In the South, thousands of slaves worked on large plantations.

Abraham Lincoln was the 16th president, elected in 1860 and re-elected in 1864. He was responsible for guiding the Union to victory in the Civil War. He ended slavery and was the first president to be assassinated.

Lincoln cherished the Declaration of Independence. He considered slavery to be a contradiction of the noble document, which contains the famous words, "all men are created equal."

Born in a Log Cabin

Abraham Lincoln was born February 12, 1809, in a one-room log cabin in Hardin County, Kentucky. His father, Thomas Lincoln, was a farmer and carpenter, and his mother, Nancy Hanks, a devoted mother to Abe and his sister, Sarah, who was two years older. A brother, Thomas, died a few days after being born in 1812. Abraham's home was small and simple. The floor of the log cabin was dirt, the door hung on leather hinges, and there was only one small window. The bathroom was an outhouse.

Abraham Lincoln was born in this log cabin in Kentucky. Most settlers during this period of American history lived in simple homes like this one. His father built the cabin from trees he cut down.

This 1844 painting is of the Fox River in Indiana. Lincoln grew up in a wild, untamed frontier area very much like this one.

In December 1816, the Lincolns moved to Indiana. Abraham wrote that his father left Kentucky "partly on account of slavery, but chiefly on account of the difficulty in land titles in Kentucky." His father heard he could buy wilderness land in Indiana from the government for little money. A Baptist, Thomas Lincoln believed it was wrong to own slaves to do the work that a man could do himself. Kentucky allowed slaves, but in Indiana all men and women were free.

A Fearsome Place

This is how Lincoln described his Indiana home: "It was a wild region, with many bears and other wild animals still in the woods [and] *the panther's scream filled the night with fear."*

A Hard Childhood

Indiana in 1816 was mostly unsettled. The Lincoln family had few neighbors and lived again in a log cabin. Lincoln mainly wore only a cloth shirt when a small child. When he was older, he wore pants and shoes made from deer hide and a cap made from the skin of a raccoon.

Sarah Bush Lincoln, Abraham's beloved stepmother, believed he would be a great man someday. A childhood friend of the young Abe once recalled, "...she wasn't goin' to have him hindered."

Abraham Lincoln's mother died when Abe was only nine. The next year his father married Sarah Bush Johnston, a widow with two girls and a boy of her own. Sarah, like his mother Nancy before, encouraged Abraham to learn to read and to dream he could do something important.

Young Abe Lincoln would often work in solitude in the wilderness. The only sounds all day long would come from the swinging of his ax, his own voice, or nature. This quietness would become a large part of his personality.

Abraham worked hard and became well-known for his skill with an ax. His father allowed neighbors to hire Abe as a worker for 25 cents a day. One chore Abe did with his ax was split trees into rails used to make fences. This is how Lincoln got the nickname "the Rail-Splitter." Abraham loved his father, but preferred reading and learning to working in the field.

Hard Work

"Abraham, though very young, was large of his age, and had an ax put into his hands at once; and from that till [he was an adult] *he was almost constantly handling that most useful instrument."*

From a campaign profile Lincoln wrote in 1860

FIGHTING FOR AN EDUCATION

For the young Abraham Lincoln, trying to attend school was not easy. He once said he learned "by littles," meaning he could only go to school occasionally. Abraham attended school for a total of one full year. In Lincoln's day, students learned lessons by repeating them over and over until they memorized them.

Abraham Lincoln
his hand and pen.
he will be good but
god knows When

Abraham Lincoln loved to practice writing. He wrote this simple verse in the early 1820s: "Abraham Lincoln, his hand and pen. he will be good but god knows when."

An army of a 10000 men having plundered a city took so much money that when it was shared among them each man had £27. I demand how much money was taken in all

Abraham Lincoln His Book

This is a page from one of Abraham's math books. The schools he attended could only teach him basic skills like reading, writing, and arithmetic.

A Frontier School

Abraham and his sister, Sarah, walked several miles to school. Their school was only one room where students of all ages were taught at the same time. Abraham often missed school because he had to help his father with farm work. Lincoln admitted he was ashamed of his lack of education: "Of course when I came of age I did not know much. Still somehow, I could read, write, and cipher [do arithmetic]; but that was all. I have not been to school since."

Abraham read every book he could find and once walked 20 miles to borrow one. His favorites included a biography of George Washington, the novel *Robinson Crusoe* by Daniel Defoe, and the Bible. Lincoln's writing style was shaped by the Bible's beautiful language. He told people, "The things I want to know are in books. My best friend is the man who'll git me a book I ain't read."

Abraham Lincoln reads by the glow from the fireplace in his family's log cabin. It seemed to those around him that he could make books tell him more than they told other people.

Making Something of Himself

In March 1830, the Lincolns moved to Illinois. They settled uncleared land on the Sangamon River near present-day Decatur. Now 21, Abraham was very tall at six feet four inches, and very strong, even though he was thin. He decided to leave home and move to New Salem, Illinois.

This illustration depicts the Lincoln family's home in Illinois. The journey from Kentucky was a harsh one, with each family member becoming ill along the way.

In New Salem, Abraham helped run a store and was the town's postmaster. He earned the title "Honest Abe" by walking several miles to return a few pennies to a customer who had paid too much. Abraham worked hard but he kept learning, too. He borrowed books from a teacher and joined a debating club to learn to speak correctly.

Lincoln's First Dollar

When he was 18, Abraham rowed two men across a river so they could board a larger boat. Both men gave him a half-dollar. "I could scarcely believe that I, a poor boy, had earned a dollar in less than a day—that by honest work I had earned a dollar. I was a more hopeful and confident being from that time."

In 1832, Abraham was a soldier for three months. He joined the Illinois militia to fight Sac and Fox Indians in the Black Hawk War. Lincoln never actually fought the Indians in a battle. Even so, in 1859 he wrote that he enjoyed his time as a soldier: "I was elected a Captain of Volunteers—a success which gave me more pleasure than any I have had since."

Politician and Lawyer

In 1834, Lincoln began studying the law in his spare time. Two years later he started work as a lawyer. He defended people accused of crimes and helped people who were in debt or divorcing. Within a few years, Lincoln was earning $1,500 a year, a good wage in the 19th century. He moved to Springfield, Illinois, in April 1837.

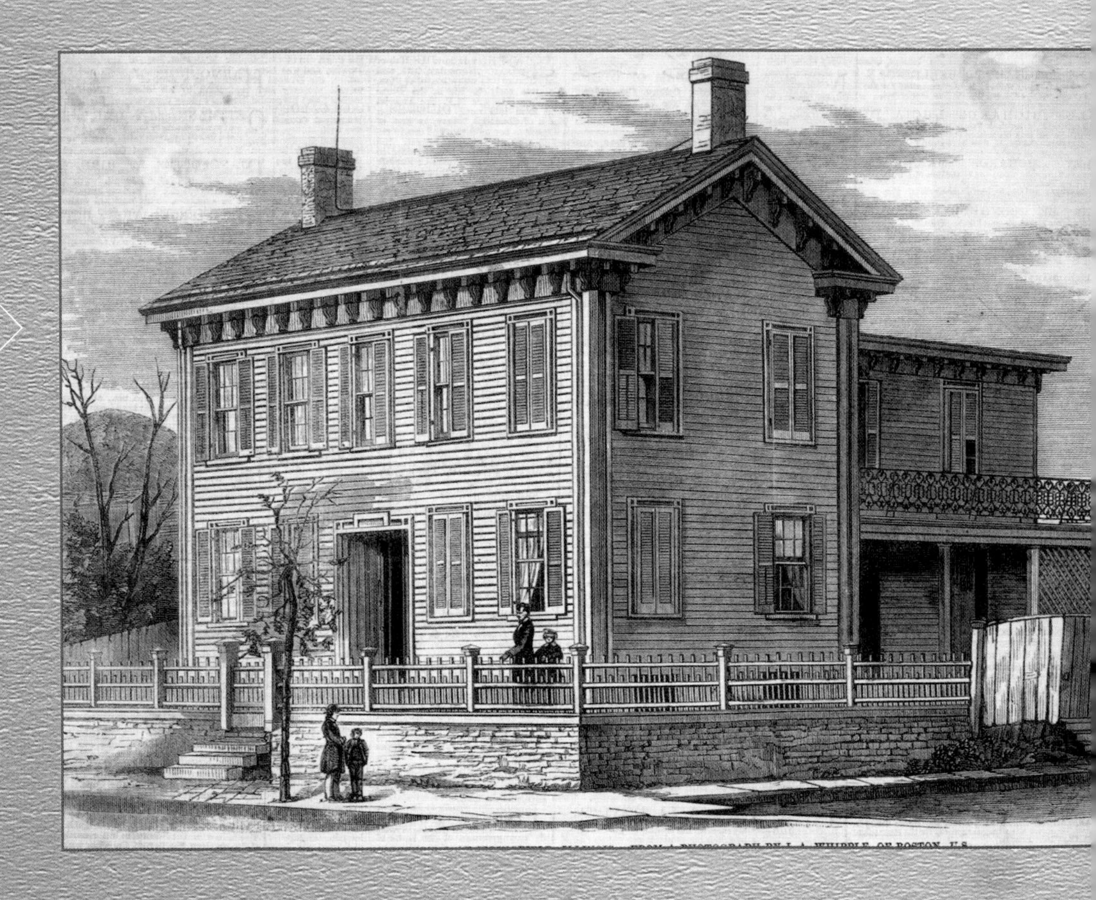

This painting from 1860 shows the home Abraham Lincoln owned in Springfield, Illinois. He lived there for many years until he was elected president and moved to Washington, D.C.

Abraham Lincoln began his career in politics as a member of the Whig Party. In 1834, he was elected to the Illinois General Assembly, a position he held for eight years. Then, in 1846, Lincoln was elected to the U.S. House of Representatives, where he was outspoken in his opposition to slavery and the Mexican War.

Political Parties

The Whig Party was formed in 1834. In the 1850s, the growing division in America over slavery led to the creation of the Republican Party. Abraham Lincoln and other people left the Whig Party and became Republicans because they wanted to fight slavery. The Whig Party collapsed because of this. The Democratic Party was strong in southern states because it supported slavery.

On November 4, 1842, Lincoln married Mary Todd, a well-to-do member of Springfield society. They would have four sons, but only Robert, their first child, would survive to adulthood.

Abraham Lincoln, his wife, Mary, and three of his sons, Thomas, Robert, and William. Lincoln was president and the Civil War was in progress when this family portrait was painted, around 1862.

The Lincoln–Douglas Debates

Lincoln left Congress in 1848 at the end of his term to work again as a lawyer. But he returned to politics in 1854, angry that Senator Stephen A. Douglas, an Illinois Democrat, wanted to allow slavery in the future states of Kansas and Nebraska if the people in those states wished it. Lincoln now quit the Whig Party and joined the new Republican Party, which opposed the spread of slavery to new areas.

A Terrible Sight

In 1855, Lincoln wrote a letter about a steamboat trip he had taken in 1841 that showed why he hated slavery: "There were, on board, ten or a dozen slaves, shackled together with irons. The sight was continual torment to me [and still has] the power of making me miserable."

This painting depicts a slave auction. The man pointing is selling the woman standing next to him.

Lincoln proposed the series of seven debates with Douglas. People from all walks of life actively participated. Sitting or standing for hours in the rain or sunshine, they shouted questions, cheered, and groaned about the issue of slavery and the future of the Union.

In 1858, Lincoln ran against Douglas for the Senate. Their seven campaign debates are considered the most dramatic and powerful ever held. The main issue was slavery, which Lincoln called "a moral, social, and political evil." Lincoln was not elected, but he became nationally famous for the power of his speeches and people began to consider him a possible presidential candidate. As many as 15,000 people had attended each debate.

LINCOLN BECOMES PRESIDENT

On February 27, 1860, Abraham Lincoln made a famous speech about slavery at the Cooper Institute in New York City. Lincoln stated his belief that slavery was wrong and that the federal government had the power to prevent it from spreading to new states and territories.

Lincoln relied on his own judgment, which often did not reflect the popular sentiments of the time.

All Free or All Slave

"A house divided against itself cannot stand. I believe this government cannot endure permanently half slave and half free."

Republican State Convention speech, June 16, 1858

In 1860, slavery was the top issue in the election for president. Northern states opposed it while southern states, which depended on slaves as workers for their economy, supported it. The Republican Party chose Lincoln as its presidential nominee. In the election on November 6, Lincoln defeated three other candidates—John C. Breckinridge, John Bell, and Stephen A. Douglas—to become president.

Whiskers

Lincoln was the first president to wear a beard. He grew it after his election because of a letter from 11-year-old Grace Bedell. The little girl wrote: "You would look a great deal better because your face is so thin. All the ladies like whiskers."

Mary Todd Lincoln in the gown she wore in 1861, when her husband was inaugurated as president.

Southern states were angry Lincoln won because they believed he would end slavery. Several immediately seceded from (left) the Union. In his inaugural address on March 4, 1861, Lincoln begged the "Confederate" states not to start war. "We must not be enemies," he said.

The Civil War

The Civil War began on April 12, 1861, less than six weeks after Lincoln became president. Fighting started when soldiers for the Confederate States of America attacked Fort Sumter in South Carolina. The North had 23 states and 21 million people. The South had only 11 states and 9 million people, and a third of them were slaves.

Fort Sumter in South Carolina. The Union had held off from entering into a war until the "rebels" attacked this federal site.

The Confederate president was Jefferson Davis. Richmond, Virginia, was the capital of the Confederacy.

Jefferson Davis was president of the Confederate States of America. In his inaugural address, he extended a warm invitation to any states that "may seek to unite their fortune with ours."

Soldiers on both sides fought in a savage war that lasted four years. There were many huge battles with names that are still famous today—Gettysburg, Antietam, Fredericksburg, and Bull Run. More Americans were killed than in any other war in U.S. history: some 360,000 Union soldiers and about 260,000 Confederates.

The Confederate states were Alabama, Arkansas, Florida, Georgia, Louisiana, Mississippi, North Carolina, South Carolina, Tennessee, Texas, and Virginia. Four southern states that allowed slavery remained in the Union: Maryland, Missouri, Delaware, and Kentucky. West Virginia—a free state—was established in 1863.

THE GREAT EMANCIPATOR

On September 22, 1862, Lincoln issued the Emancipation Proclamation. This document abolished slavery in slave states in rebellion against the Union. The proclamation did not apply to slaves in states loyal to the Union. Even so, the proclamation earned Lincoln the nickname "The Great Emancipator."

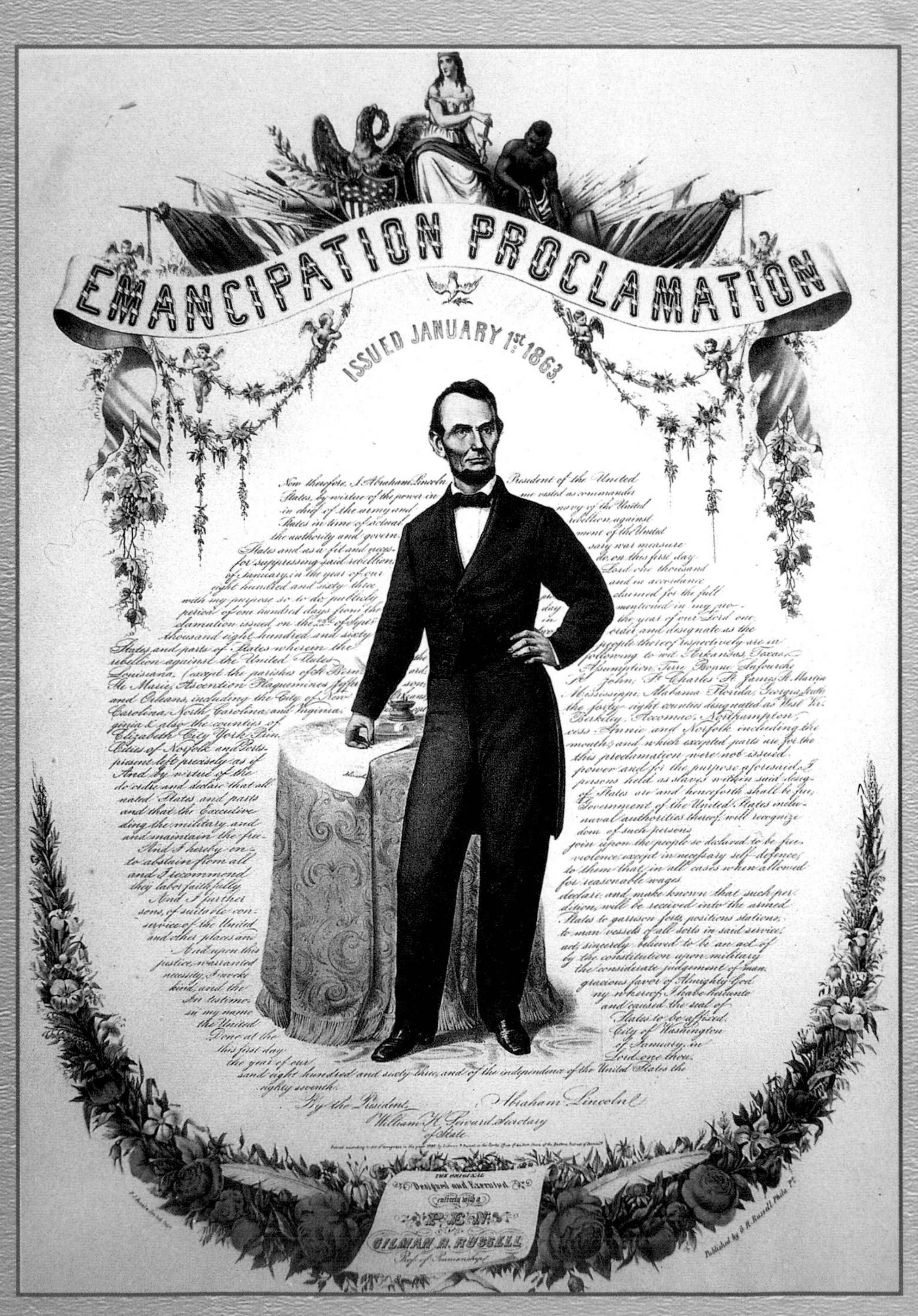

Lincoln, who rarely wrote his full name, slowly and carefully signed what would become one of the most important documents in U.S. history. When the Emancipation Proclamation was published in newspapers in major Union cities, salutes of 100 guns were fired.

African-American Soldiers

More than 180,000 African Americans joined the Union army. They came from both southern and northern states. They fought in almost every battle of the long, bloody war, and more than 68,000 died battling for freedom.

By freeing the slaves there, Lincoln hoped that the Confederacy would fall apart. Lincoln knew that the Confederacy needed its slaves to raise food, dig trenches, and work. As Union armies defeated those of the Confederacy, the former slaves would become Union allies and soldiers.

Slavery and Democracy

Lincoln believed slavery could not exist in a democracy: "As I would not be a slave, so I would not be a master. This expresses my idea of democracy. Whatever differs from this, to the extent of the difference, is no democracy."

Winning the War

Lincoln had to run for re-election during the Civil War. On November 8, 1864, the Republican president beat George B. McClellan, a Democrat and the former commander of the Union forces, by more than 400,000 votes.

This poster promotes Lincoln's re-election. His victory proved that the people of the Union, however weary from the war, believed it should continue.

The Union won the Civil War because it had more soldiers, newer weapons, and better supplies. Another reason was that Abraham Lincoln was a strong and capable war leader. The Confederacy's greatest general was Robert E. Lee. On April 9, 1865, Lee, realizing the Confederacy could never win, surrendered at Appomattox Court House, Virginia. The war was over. The Union had won.

Rebuilding a Country

"With malice toward none; with charity for all...to bind up the nation's wounds [and] to do all which may achieve and cherish a just and lasting peace."

Lincoln's second inaugural address, March 4, 1865

Lincoln visits the front lines during the Civil War. To the left is Major Allan Pinkerton and to the right General John McClernand. Lincoln took an active role in helping plan strategy for the war.

Life in the South was changed forever. With the Union restored, Lincoln now had to make the southern states part of the nation again. This process became known as Reconstruction. In December 1865, the Thirteenth Amendment to the U.S. Constitution made slavery illegal in the United States.

Personal Losses

The Civil War had set brother against brother. Even the Lincoln family was personally involved in the conflict: Lincoln's wife lost her three brothers in the war. All were fighting for the Confederacy.

Assassination at Ford's Theatre

On April 14, 1865, the U.S. flag was raised over Fort Sumter again. That night, President Abraham Lincoln and his wife, Mary, went to Ford's Theatre in Washington, D.C. to see a play, *Our American Cousin*. During the play, actor John Wilkes Booth sneaked into the president's box and shot Lincoln in the back of the head. Some witnesses heard Booth shout, "The South is avenged." Lincoln died at 7:22 A.M. the next morning.

John Wilkes Booth felt that by assassinating Lincoln he was saving America from dishonor. He wanted the world to know that he was responsible for the act and was sure that he would be honored for it. Ford's Theatre is pictured above.

JOHN WILKES BOOTH

John Wilkes Booth was born in Maryland. He was from a family of famous actors. Booth succeeded in escaping from Ford's Theatre after shooting Lincoln, but on April 26 he was surrounded and the barn he was hiding in was set afire. He was shot and killed in the gun battle that followed. The three other men and one woman who helped plan the assassination were hanged.

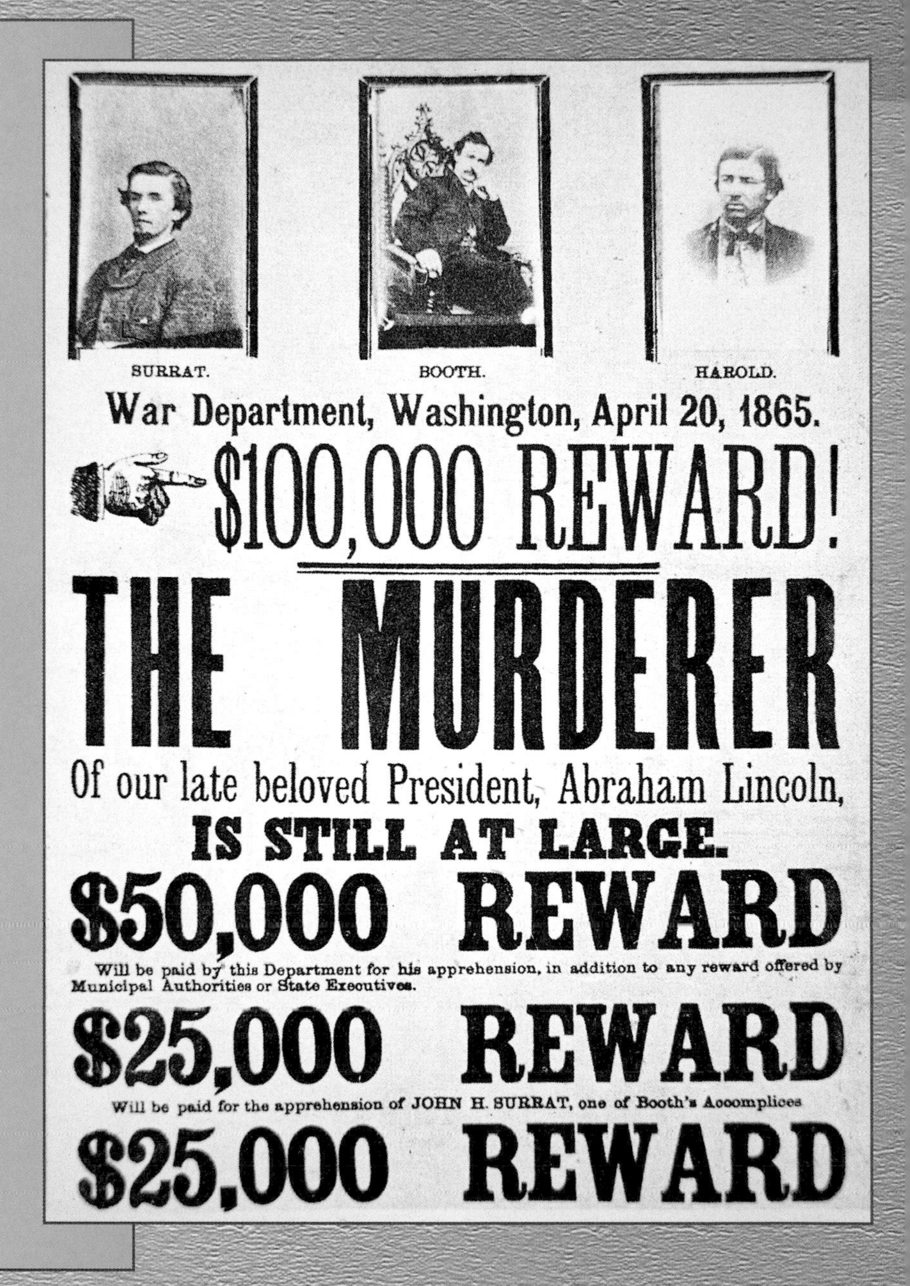

SURRAT. BOOTH. HAROLD.

War Department, Washington, April 20, 1865.

$100,000 REWARD!

THE MURDERER

Of our late beloved President, Abraham Lincoln,

IS STILL AT LARGE.

$50,000 REWARD

Will be paid by this Department for his apprehension, in addition to any reward offered by Municipal Authorities or State Executives.

$25,000 REWARD

Will be paid for the apprehension of JOHN H. SURRAT, one of Booth's Accomplices

$25,000 REWARD

When Lincoln was killed, many Union supporters wanted revenge on the South. But the assassination was a conspiracy involving only Booth and a few other people.

Lincoln's funeral was held at the White House on April 19. Tens of thousands of people came to honor him. His body was then taken by train to Springfield, Illinois, where he was buried there on May 4 in Oak Ridge Cemetery.

Lincoln's Fame Lives On Today

More books have been written about Abraham Lincoln than any other American. Lincoln is revered because he accomplished so many great things. As president during the Civil War, a critical period in American history, he preserved the Union. Lincoln also stood up for the rights of all people by making slavery illegal.

People line the streets of Washington, D.C., to bid a tearful farewell to Abraham Lincoln. His body is in a casket on the small military wagon that is being pulled by horses. Much of the nation mourned the death of this great man.

The Lincoln Memorial

The Lincoln Memorial in Washington, D.C., was completed in 1922. Because Lincoln valued freedom and equality, his memorial has been the site of many civil rights protests. The most significant was on August 28, 1963, when the Reverend Martin Luther King, Jr., delivered his famous "I Have a Dream" speech. King's dream was to end discrimination against African Americans.

Americans continue to honor Lincoln today. His face is on the $5 bill and the penny, and he is one of four presidents whose image was carved on Mount Rushmore in South Dakota. His birthday is observed every February with George Washington's as a national holiday.

Most importantly, Lincoln lives on in the hearts of Americans. He is considered a symbol of the struggle for equality and freedom.

No Fool

"You can fool some of the people all of the time, and all of the people some of the time, but you can't fool all of the people all of the time."

Abraham Lincoln

Timeline

February 12, 1809–Abraham Lincoln is born in Hardin County, Kentucky.

December 1816–Lincoln's family moves to Indiana.

March 1830–Lincoln's family moves to Illinois.

April 1832–Lincoln joins the Illinois Militia during the Black Hawk War.

August 1834–Lincoln wins election to the Illinois General Assembly.

April 15, 1837–Lincoln moves to Springfield, Illinois. He lives there until 1861.

November 4, 1842–Lincoln marries Mary Todd in Springfield, Illinois.

August 2, 1846–Lincoln elected to U.S. House of Representatives.

June 1858–Lincoln runs against Stephen A. Douglas for the Senate.

February 27, 1860–Lincoln gives the Cooper Institute speech.

May 18, 1860–Lincoln is nominated as the Republican candidate for president.

November 6, 1860–Lincoln is elected president.

March 4, 1861–Lincoln is inaugurated as the 16th president.

April 12, 1861–Confederates fire on Fort Sumter, South Carolina, to begin the Civil War.

September 22, 1862–Lincoln issues the Emancipation Proclamation.

November 19, 1863–Lincoln delivers the Gettysburg Address.

November 8, 1864–Lincoln is re-elected president.

March 4, 1865–Lincoln is inaugurated for a second term.

April 9, 1865–Robert E. Lee surrenders.

April 14, 1865–Lincoln is shot in the head by John Wilkes Booth.

April 15, 1865–Lincoln dies of gunshot wounds.

May 4, 1865–Lincoln is buried at Oak Ridge Cemetery in Springfield.

December 6, 1865–The 13th Amendment, ending slavery, is ratified.

Glossary

Amendment (uh-MEND-muhnt) A change in the Constitution.

Assassinate (uh-SASS-uh-nate) To kill someone for political reasons.

Capital (kap-UH-tul) The city in which a state or national government meets.

Confederate States of America (also the Confederacy) (kuhn-FED-ur-uht STATES uhv uh-MER-uh-kuh) The states that seceded from the Union and fought together in the Civil War.

Congress (KONG-griss) The name for the two houses of the federal legislature: the House of Representatives and the Senate.

Constitution (kon-stuh-TOO-shuhn) The document that sets out the basic principles of government for the U.S.

Democracy (di-MOK-ruh-see) A form of government in which the people elect the officials who govern them.

Emancipate (ee-MAN-si-pate) To free someone.

House of Representatives (HOUSS uhv rep-ri-ZEN-tuh-tivz) The group of federal lawmakers elected from districts within each state.

Illinois General Assembly (il-luh-NOY GEN-ur-uhl uh-SEM-blee) The legislature for the state of Illinois.

Inauguration (in-aw-gyuh-RAY-shuhn) The ceremony in which a person officially becomes president.

Postmaster (POHST-mass-tur) The person responsible for making sure the mail is delivered in a community.

Secede (si-SEED) To decide as a state to leave the United States.

Senate (SEN-it) The group of federal legislators elected from each state. Each state has two senators.

Slave (SLAYV) A person who is owned as property by someone else.

Union (YOON-yuhn) A nickname for the United States; also, the states that did not secede and fought together in the Civil War.

Further Reading and Information

Books to Read

Cary, Barbara. *Meet Abraham Lincoln (Landmark Books).* New York: Random House Inc., 2001.

Jacobs, William Jay. *Lincoln.* New York: Charles Scribner's Sons, 1991.

Kunhardt, Edith. *Honest Abe.* New York: Greenwillow Books, 1993.

Mcneer, May. *America's Abraham Lincoln.* Lakeville, CT: Grey Castle Press, 1991.

Sullivan, George. *In Their Own Words: Abraham Lincoln.* New York: Scholastic Reference, 2001.

Turner, Ann Warren. *Abe Lincoln Remembers.* New York: HarperCollins Juvenile Books, 2000.

Usel, T. M. *Abraham Lincoln: A Photo-Illustrated Biography.* Mankato, MN: Bridgestone Books, 1996.

Woods, Andrew. *Young Abraham Lincoln: Log-Cabin President (First-Start Biographies).* Mahwah, NJ: Troll Communications, 1992.

Videos

Biography—Abraham Lincoln. A&E Entertainment, 1997.

Lincoln. PBS Home Video, 1995.

The Lincoln Assassination. A&E Entertainment, 1995.

The American Experience—Abraham and Mary Lincoln: A House Divided. PBS Home Video, 2001.

INDEX